T0278148

PAST & PRESENT

CLINTON AND KIRKLAND

OPPOSITE: This past image shows a horse-drawn carriage on West Park Row in the village of Clinton. This unpaved-street view was photographed around 1910. The camera is set up on Kirkland Avenue, which was then named Water Street. (Courtesy of the Clinton Historical Society.)

CLINTON AND KIRKLAND

Zach Lewis
Foreword by Richard L. Williams

This book is dedicated to all the students who were in my English classes over the years. You inspire me. Thank you for the privilege of being your teacher. I'll always be your biggest supporter.

Published by Arcadia Publishing
Charleston, South Carolina

Printed in the United States of America

For all general information, please contact Arcadia Publishing:
Telephone 843-853-2070
Fax 843-853-0044
E-mail sales@arcadiapublishing.com

Visit us on the Internet at www.arcadiapublishing.com

ON THE FRONT COVER: Since the first shop opened on West Park Row, the area has been a business center. Locally owned shops, restaurants, and businesses continue to line West Park Row to this day. The past photograph shows a corner store at Hogan's Corner. Today, the corner spot is home to the popular Utica Coffee Roasting Co. (Past, courtesy of Clinton Historical Society; present, photograph by the author.)

ON THE BACK COVER: While leaving the small hamlet of Deansboro south of Clinton, drivers are met with this township sign. The town of Kirkland derives its name from Rev. Samuel Kirkland, an instrumental figure in the entwined histories of Clinton and Kirkland. (Past, courtesy of Clinton Historical Society.)

CONTENTS

Foreword   vii
Acknowledgments   viii
Introduction   ix

1   Around the Village Green   11

2.   College Street and College Hill Road   27

3.   Side Streets and Other Roads   53

FOREWORD

Local history buffs in Oneida County will find Zach Lewis's new book full of photographs showing major features of the town of Kirkland and, within it, the village of Clinton.

The story of any small community can be aptly told with photographs of how landscapes looked 150 years ago and how they look today. Whether a church, a home, a farm silo, a civic building, or a school, Zach has provided the past and present in the nearly 170 images to follow.

Local readers will view these pictures with interest and will be able to identify them quickly. Many drive or walk right by the places depicted in the images daily and probably wonder about the history of the location. Each set of images tells a story of the past and the present and tells the story of change in a small upstate New York community.

As Kirkland and Clinton public historian, I have witnessed and written about much change in my over 80 years, and I salute Zach for collecting and taking these pictures for Arcadia's Past & Present series to keep these memories alive for today and future residents.

—Richard L. Williams

ACKNOWLEDGMENTS

I owe the biggest debt of gratitude to the Clinton Historical Society (CHS). Without support from members of CHS and the board, this book would not have been possible. Also, thank you, Hamilton College, for allowing me to do research in your archives. I was able to find some amazing photographs in the historic college's collection.

The biggest thank you goes to Clinton and Kirkland historian Richard L. Williams. Without his extensive and expert knowledge and documentation of local historical events through his many books, this printed work would not have materialized. His commitment to this area's history has not only benefited me but also many other writers. He was kind enough to write the foreword to this book and check the content accuracy on the following pages. I am extremely grateful and immensely thankful.

Had I not listened closely to the years of stories from my grandfather and Clintonian Carl Christ, this book idea would not have crossed my mind. My grandfather's firsthand experience of living and working in Clinton and Kirkland fueled my passion for this area's history from an early age. My family's deep roots in the community date back generations. The family business, which operated under the name of Christ Bros., delivered ice and milk to area residents throughout the early to mid-1900s.

One last acknowledgment is to the *Waterville Times,* the official newspaper of Clinton and Kirkland. Since the closure of the *Clinton Courier* in 2015, which provided weekly news for nearly 170 years, the *Times* has been providing Clinton and Kirkland residents with up-to-date community news. When I was asked to join the *Times* as a Clinton correspondent, I was extremely honored to be able to add to the documentation of historical events in the town I love. Thanks, Patty!

Courier articles from yesteryear proved vital when writing this book. Also invaluable were the authors before me who tackled the documentation of Clinton and Kirkland history. I would also like to thank every individual who helped with this journey along the way. This book has been a dream come true.

The past photographs that appear in this book were exclusively acquired from the Clinton Historical Society unless otherwise noted. The author took all the present photographs.

INTRODUCTION

The village of Clinton and the town of Kirkland can be traced back to 1766, when Rev. Samuel Kirkland started missionary work among the Indigenous peoples of the area, the Onyota'a:ka (Oneida, People of the Standing Stone). Kirkland worked just a few miles west of Clinton in present-day Oneida Castle. In 1768, the Fort Stanwix Treaty Line of Property was established. A stone monument at the foot of College Hill Road marked the line that separated Indigenous land from the colonies.

In 1776, the Declaration of Independence was signed, and in 1777, the Mohawk Valley was the site of a bloody battle that took place at Oriskany—approximately 10 miles from Clinton. Because of Kirkland's work during the American Revolutionary War as an intermediary for colonists and the area's Indigenous peoples, he was granted land in 1788—Kirkland's Patent— between Harding Road and Skyline Drive. During the war, the Oneidas sided with the Americans. (A statue named *Allies in War; Partners in Peace* is displayed at the Smithsonian's National Museum of the American Indian honoring this alliance.)

In the early 1790s, Reverend Kirkland had the idea for a school that would be accessible to Indigenous youth and the children of surrounding settlers. According to *Oneida County: An Illustrated History*, a publication by the Oneida County History Center, Kirkland presented his plan to Pres. George Washington and Secretary of the Treasury Alexander Hamilton, both showing support. Hamilton's name was used for the academy, and he became one of the school's first trustees. The Hamilton-Oneida Academy started in 1793.

The academy was later chartered as Hamilton College in 1812, making it New York's third-oldest college. Kirkland and Oneida chief Shenendoah (the multiple spellings of the name include Schenando and Skenandoa) became close friends from years of working together. Kirkland, who died in 1808, and Skenandoa, who died at the age of 110 in 1816, are buried next to each other in the Hamilton College Cemetery. It was Skenandoa's wish to be buried near his friend Kirkland.

The next person in the story of Clinton was Capt. Moses Foote. He, along with seven other families, settled in the area that is now Clinton in 1787. The settlement was named after New York's first governor, George Clinton. Most of the families who settled in Clinton at that time were from Connecticut.

Resulting from a population increase in the area, new towns and counties were formed. The Clinton settlement was a part of Kirkland, which was in the town of German Flatts until 1788. A few years later in 1792, Kirkland became part of the town of Paris. "The first meeting of the new Town of Paris was held in Clinton on April 2, 1793, in the house of Moses Foote, Esquire," according to *Kirkland Since 1827* by Richard L. Williams.

A few notable events that took place in the early days of Clinton's history included the mining of iron ore in 1797. Oneida County, which now includes the town of Kirkland, was formed in 1798. Clinton's first post office opened in 1802. The small factory Clinton Woolen

Manufacturing Company opened in 1810. The Manchester (now Kirkland) Post Office opened in 1815. In 1819, founder Foote died and was buried in the Old Burying Ground, Clinton's oldest cemetery.

In 1827, the town of Kirkland was officially established, giving the municipality a governing body. The village of Clinton was incorporated in 1843. The town of Kirkland included the hamlets of Chuckery, Clark's Mills (now Clark Mills), Franklin (now Franklin Springs), and Manchester (now Kirkland).

From the days of the early founders, the Village Green has been the central location of community activities and bustled with business as years went by. From food markets and bakeries to music halls and hotels, the business district has been lively. Mills and small factories popped up around Clinton and Kirkland in the early years, some near the mighty Oriskany Creek to utilize its waterpower. Agriculture was a part of the area's early economy. There was also the mining of abundant hematite ore. Although the area was rich with this ore—so much so, in fact, village roads of the day were noticeably red from the transport of the reddish-brown mineral—the mining operation was inconsistent and did not prove to be the most robust of ventures.

As more houses were built and streets developed around Clinton, history was unfolding in every corner of the village. For example, a child by the name of Stephen, who lived on Utica Street, would later grow up to be the president of the United States. We know Stephen today as Pres. Grover Cleveland—the only US president, so far, to serve two nonconsecutive terms in office. Or at the top of Williams Street, on the location of the estate with four white pillars, was the home of the female division of the Clinton Liberal Institute, where Red Cross founder Clara Barton completed her education. And atop College Hill Road, where Hamilton College is situated, some of the most famous leaders and thinkers were educated, including native son Elihu Root, who was not only the 38th US secretary of state, 41st secretary of war, and a US senator from New York, but he also received the Nobel Peace Prize in 1912.

In recent years, Clinton and Kirkland have continued to make historic headlines. In 2018, because of Clinton's deep ice hockey history that dates to the 1920s, the village was named Kraft Hockeyville USA. By winning the title, a professional National Hockey League (NHL) game was played at the Clinton Arena, and $150,000 for repairs and upgrades to the ice rink was awarded. In 2023, the village and town were the recipients of a New York State Downtown Revitalization Initiative grant, which jointly provides the municipalities $10 million to be used toward improving and modernizing various locations in the village and town.

The history that has occurred—and continues to take place—in this small community is significant. Throughout this book, various buildings, streets, and landmarks from around Clinton and Kirkland will be highlighted. It was not possible to fit all the rare photographs found of Clinton and Kirkland in this book. For more details on the village of Clinton and the town of Kirkland, please visit the Clinton Historical Society at 1 Fountain Street in Clinton.

AROUND THE VILLAGE GREEN

Since Clinton's beginning, the Village Green, shown on the left side of this photograph, has been a community focal point. Businesses around the Village Green have provided fundamentals for generations. In this past image, cars can be seen parked for an event on the green. The car pictured in the middle would cause a stir today as West Park Row is now a one-way street in the opposite direction. (Past, courtesy of Clinton Historical Society.)

The Founder's Monument at the south end of the Village Green marks the distance between Utica and Clinton and displays the names of the original settlers. The monument was originally placed there in 1869. Below the "Nine Miles to Utica" inscription, Moses Foote is listed as a founder of the Clinton. Foote's first house was across from the monument on the corner of Williams and College Streets.

Today, like in years past, the Village Green has been used for various activities and events. In the past photograph, the Founder's Monument can be seen near a man sitting under a tree while kids play in the distance. Annual events like the Clinton Art and Music Festival, Shoppers' Stroll, farmers market, and various holiday parades continue to keep people gathering on the green.

PARK - CLINTON, N. Y.

The Village Green's central fountain features a bronze statue of a girl standing on a sea urchin, dating back to 1939 when the Houghton Seminary Alumnae Association donated the memorial. It is said the hand of the statue is pointing toward the former seminary's location on Chestnut Street, in existence from 1861 to 1903. A similar sea urchin statue by Edward Berge is displayed at Johns Hopkins University.

The corner of West Park Row and College Street was once known as the Foote Block because it was the site of a hotel and boardinghouse owned by founder Moses Foote. This past photograph is one of the earliest known images of the village from the 1850s. A fire destroyed the block in 1872. The first store on the left was known as Hogan's Corner under Timothy Hogan's ownership through the early 1950s. In the 1990s, Hemstrought's Bakery thrived at that corner spot. Since 2017, Utica Coffee Roasting Co. has occupied the location. Few call it Hogan's Corner today.

From the Village Green, here is a glimpse at the business district of the village. The architecture of the buildings in the past and present images has largely remained unchanged over the years. From stores like Gorton's to Grand Union to the Children's Corner and even an opera house, the buildings in these photographs have seen a variety of businesses flourish. On this block in 1887, the Bristol-Myers Company started as the Clinton Pharmaceutical Company.

This view shows the beginning of North Park Row, the location of the old Sherman Block. A popular bakery in the village was the Clinton Home Bakery, which is pictured in the past image. During the 1880s to 1926, the Sherman Block housed a post office. The brick building on the far right in each photograph is the Clinton Fire Department. (Past, courtesy of Hamilton College.)

When Pres. Grover Cleveland—who lived on Utica Street for a few years as a boy—arrived in Clinton on July 13, 1887, for the village's centennial celebration, the area was abuzz with excitement. One of the locations Cleveland stopped was at the decorated house of Judge Othniel S. Williams, now the Alexander Hamilton Institute for the Study of Western Civilization. For many years, this location operated as the Alexander Hamilton Inn. Williams was Kirkland's first supervisor.

The Burns Agency has been in business for a century. Up until recently, the company was independently owned by the Burns family. A few months prior to publishing this book, the Burns Agency was acquired by a local neighboring insurance agency. The house from which the Burns Agency operates once served as a schoolhouse in the late 19th century. Clinton had so many private schools, academies, and seminaries that it earned the nickname of "schooltown."

The Clinton Fire Department has operated on North Park Row since 1921. Dawes Meat Market, which was situated behind the firehouse, faced Kirkland Avenue until it ceased operation in 1947. Prior to the North Park Row firehouse, the Clinton Fire Department worked out of a location on Williams Street. The Clinton Fire Department operates with volunteer firefighters.

Ralph S. Lumbard Memorial Town Hall, 100 North Park Row, is one of the most recognizable buildings in Clinton. Prior to this stately structure, the site was home to the Park House, a tavern and hotel built in 1800 and torn down in 1899. Lumbard Hall was constructed on the site in 1926 and housed the Clinton Post Office for many years. This past photograph was taken in August 1926. The Village of Clinton uses offices in the building today.

The line of houses and buildings along East Park Row now includes the Kirkland Art Center, housed in a former Methodist Episcopal Church from 1842. The first village schoolhouse stood at 9 East Park Row in the late 1790s before moving to the corner of Kellogg and Mulberry Streets. Pres. Millard Fillmore's brother was an early teacher at the school, according to *The History of Clinton Square* by Mary Bell Dever.

AROUND THE VILLAGE GREEN

Highlighted behind the line of Clinton firefighters below and disguised by trees above is the present-day Clinton Historical Society building. The 1832 church centered in the past image served as the Baptist Church of Christ and is the village's oldest surviving church structure. CHS acquired it in 1993 for its headquarters. Also in the past photograph on the right is the former Park Hotel.

This past photograph features the historic Park Hotel, built around 1883. The sign on the building in the past image displays Willard House, named after Russell Willard, who originally established it as a hotel. After an ownership change, the building became known as the Park Hotel by the start of the 1900s. It was a staple in the community until 1961, when a fire destroyed the building. The present image shows what the area looks like today—a village parking lot.

AROUND THE VILLAGE GREEN

This unassuming 1901 building has a long history. Between the former Park Hotel and Stone Presbyterian Church stands the O.W. Kennedy Block. It was originally an office for a hop business. In 1906, it was transformed into an ice cream shop, shown in the past image. The location also served as a car dealership, an appliance store, a shoe repair shop, a dentist's office, and even housed two overflow elementary classrooms. Today, a flower shop and vintage clothing store operate from the location.

Fire caused significant disruptions in early Clinton, notably impacting South Park Row. The Congregational Church has roots dating to 1791. The construction of the "Old Stone Church" happened around 1835, becoming Presbyterian in 1864. A major 1876 blaze led to the reconstruction of Stone Presbyterian Church in 1878. This rare past stereoscopic image shows the prominent steeple, removed in 1923 for safety. Once the church's choir director, Thomas Hastings wrote the famous hymn "Rock of Ages." (Past, courtesy of Hamilton College.)

CHAPTER

2

COLLEGE STREET AND COLLEGE HILL ROAD

College Street serves as the central artery connecting many of the village's side streets. It is also a bustling street during holidays. Parades for Veterans Day, Halloween, Shoppers' Stroll, and various other events stick to the College Street route. In this 1890 photograph, Smyth Hook and Ladder Company is seen marching past the corner of Williams and College Streets during the Fireman's Parade. The H.J. Allen & Sons Hardware store is the building behind the marchers near the Stone Presbyterian Church.

27

Alteri's Restaurant has been a village favorite since Valentine's Day of 1953. The establishment's award-winning food has remained unchanged for 70 years, which keeps patrons returning. A fire destroyed the original 1883 building that housed Alteri's 10 years after the restaurant opened. However, it was rebuilt, and Alteri's, known locally as a popular hockey hangout, is still family-owned to this day.

The row of buildings opposite Alteri's housed a variety of establishments over the years, including a tavern, apothecary shop, barber, grocery store, and, in the 1800s, a livery stable. A sign for the livery is centered in this past image from 1896. By the late 1910s, the livery stable was growing obsolete as automobile usage increased. Today, the large opening shown in the past photograph has been replaced with smaller doors and different businesses.

Next door to the building that once was the livery stable is a structure that mimics other buildings on the block; it features both residential and commercial space. In recent years, this building on College Street was home to Bitteker's Electric, a business that was in operation for over five decades. The location was once an ice-cream shop and is now a nail salon.

Directly across from a one-time electronics store once stood the Cottage Hotel. The *Clinton Courier* reported that this past photograph was snapped in 1885, a year after the brick building to the right was constructed. This brick building is prominent in the present image. In 1902, the hotel became a pub named Dempsey's and operated through the 1940s. In 1959, the building was demolished. Today, it is a village parking lot.

Today's Owens-Pavlot & Rogers Funeral Service, Inc., at 35 College Street, is next door to the brick building previously mentioned. It was a doctor's residence before being acquired for use as a funeral home in the 1930s. Early clockmaker Timothy Barns, who cast the first church bell in Clinton, lived and worked out of a location behind the funeral home site. Barns's 800-pound bell was hung in 1804 at the Old White Meeting House, predating the first "Old Stone Church."

This building at 32 College Street has hosted several businesses through the decades, ranging from a laundromat to a national sandwich chain. In Clinton, the Burns family name has been associated with a variety of businesses like the Burns Agency from chapter one. Owen J. Burns, also known as "O.J.," operated a market in this very building for generations, remaining in the family from the 1880s until it closed in 1958.

This 1970s past photograph from College Street shows a gas and service station that was in operation for over 40 years. Today, the building is home to a pizzeria. An interesting detail in these photographs is the house behind the pizzeria on neighboring Marvin Street. The house showcases Gothic Revival–style eaves, which can be seen in the upper-left corner of the images. Similar design features can be found at St. James Episcopal Church on Williams Street.

Another building that has hosted a variety of businesses is located at 34 College Street. Throughout the years, it has been the site of an antique store, coffeehouse, tattoo business, hair salon, and even a magic shop. Before being used for commercial purposes, it served as the residence of Ozias Marvin, an early Clinton settler and Revolutionary War veteran, buried in the Old Burying Ground. This is one of the village's oldest structures.

Next to one of Clinton's oldest structures is this icon in red. Taverns and bars have popped up and fizzled in this area, but one that has endured is Don's Rok. In 2023, the bar changed hands and now goes by the Rok. The building was originally used as a grocery store when it was constructed in 1864. The building's distinctive shape is based on its proximity to the Chenango Canal and subsequent railroad system.

Looking west on College Street from the corner of the Rok shows a section of the New York, Ontario & Western Railway. In the 1920 image, the Keith Block can be seen to the right, existing from the 1860s until 1961. Across the street is a building with an angled side, dating back to 1864, constructed for use alongside the Chenango Canal. The canal was on the west side of the building, while the railroad was on the east side.

On the corner of College Street and Chenango Avenue was the site of the Keith Block. By the late 1960s, all the structures associated with the block had been torn down, and various businesses operated here, like the gas station seen in the past photograph. The most recent business was a bank kiosk, which was also later torn down. Today, it is an empty lot.

This is another angle of the former Keith Block. In the past image, there is construction taking place on the site of the demolished block. A popular local bakery named Holland Farms opened in 1963 at this spot next to the Rok. By April 1987, the Holland Farms building was razed to make room for a new Clinton Post Office, which opened at 40 College Street in March 1990.

Flooding has occurred on multiple occasions in the history of Clinton and Kirkland, and it is not just the Oriskany Creek that floods the area. Small local streams have been known to flood village and town roadways and properties. The current culvert indicates the place where the Chenango Canal crossed College Street. While dry most of the year, heavy rain occasionally causes what remains of the extinct canal to fill with water and flood surroundings.

In the early 1930s, the 15 one-room schools in the area were consolidated into the Clinton Central School District. The bell tower is a distinct feature of the school and can be seen from College Street. The site of the centralized school has educational roots as it was home to Cottage Seminary from 1862 to 1898. Some of the trees on the campus today are remnants from the seminary's time in operation.

The Kirkland Town Library opened on December 11, 1901, at 55½ College Street. The library started operating out of the former location of the off-campus Hamilton College 1871 Sigma Phi fraternity house. The day after the library opened, on December 12, the *Clinton Courier* reported that Clintonians celebrated their first taste of advanced transportation—a trolley car. Before moving to their current locations, the Kirkland Art Center and Clinton Historical Society used rooms upstairs at the library.

Although a beautiful sight, the late-1800s stone bridge with arches on College Street proved too narrow to handle flood debris. The old bridge, in effect, became a dam during early-spring thaws. At times, dynamite was used to clear the blockages of ice and fallen trees around the arches of the bridge. A historical marker near the bridge indicates that the first gristmill was built near this area in 1787, utilizing its proximity to Oriskany Creek.

One example of the flooding issue in Clinton occurred in June 1890, when heavy rainfall caused the Oriskany Creek to overflow, inundating College Street and surrounding roads. The *Clinton Courier* reported that all village streets were underwater, with some residents needing to use small boats to get to safety. The past photograph shows College Street flooded in the 20th century due to the Oriskany. The house centered in each photograph was torn down in 2023 and replaced with new construction.

Stone marking the line of Property between the American Colonies and the Six Nations, fixed by treaty at Fort Stanwix, Nov. 5, 1768. Clinton, N. Y.

Do you on the remember this way to College Hill.

Mama was delighted with her outing. School closed this day. Will write soon.

Arrived home safely 5:15 P. M. Mama & Papa came about six. Bruth

Near the intersection where College Street ends and College Hill Road begins stands a stone monument marking the Fort Stanwix Treaty of 1768 Line of Property, separating Indigenous land from the colonies. Placed in 1885 by the Hamilton College class of 1887, the stone has the inscription, "The Line of Property Between the American Colonies and the Six Nations." The Six Nations include the Mohawk, Oneida, Tuscarora, Onondaga, Cayuga, and Seneca tribes.

The first distinct structure seen when traveling up College Hill is the stone arbor. It has long functioned as a resting spot for those ascending the incline as it is situated at the midway point of College Hill. A wooden structure previously occupied this location until it was replaced by a stone arbor built in memory of a student from the class of 1894 who passed away. In these past and present photographs, the camera view is directed downhill.

Tucked away off College Hill lies the Hamilton College Cemetery, where Samuel Kirkland and Oneida chief Shenendoah are laid to rest. In the past image, a ceremony is occurring in front of the grave markers for Kirkland and Shenendoah (spelled "Schenando" on the marker). Many notable Hamilton College professors and past presidents have been buried in the cemetery since it was established in 1820, including Nobel Prize laureate and alumnus Elihu Root and various members of his family. (Past, courtesy of author's collection.)

The Hamilton College Chapel, a unique three-story chapel that opened in 1827, is a gem on campus that shines so brightly it can be seen from miles away. A clock system was installed in 1877, with the original chapel bell set up in 1899. The chapel received electricity in 1907, and in 1972, it was added to the National Register of Historic Places.

A distinguished feature adorning the chapel is what Hamilton College refers to as a "quilled cupola." The chapel topper even became part of the school's logo design in 2002. In 2021, repairs were made to the aged steeple. The chapel remains an integral part of the school, with various campus meetings and special events held there. Some residents have used the chapel as a wedding venue.

This statue of Alexander Hamilton faces the chapel. Samuel Kirkland presented his idea for an academy that educated both Oneida youth and children of settlers to George Washington and Alexander Hamilton in 1793. They supported it. Hamilton's name was used for the academy, and he served as an early trustee. The Oneida-Hamilton Academy became Hamilton College in 1812. The statue was a 1918 gift from Utica philanthropist Thomas R. Proctor. In 2005, a ceremony was held to commemorate the statue's base lighting upgrade.

The top of College Hill offers a stunning view of the east. The Elihu Root House is not far from this spot on the hill. Elihu's daughter Edith Root Grant and her husband Ulysses S. Grant III, grandson of the US president, once lived in the home. Hamilton College later purchased the building and renovated it for administration offices. College Hill was not paved until the early 1920s, making it an even harder trek uphill by foot or horse and wagon.

These photographs show one of the most serene places on the Hamilton College campus. Situated behind the Elihu Root House is the horticulturally diverse Root Glen. It not only features walking trails, but it is also host to around 65 species of trees and multiple species of plants and flowers, according to the Hamilton College website. The well-kept trails in Root Glen are frequented by both students and community members.

SIDE STREETS
AND OTHER ROADS

This 1920 photograph captures Kellogg Street's sharp curve and the efforts taken to make it visible. The street derives its name from the Kellogg brothers, Amos and Aaron, who arrived in Clinton in 1787. Aaron Kellogg's farmhouse stood at the corner of Kellogg and Mulberry Streets. Hiram Huntington Kellogg, Aaron's son, was born in Clinton in 1803. After graduating from Hamilton College, he established the Young Ladies Domestic Seminary on Kellogg Street before the abolitionist became Knox College's first president in 1841.

The building at the corner of College and Williams Streets was constructed by William Onyan and was known as the Onyan Block. It is now commonly referred to as the Allen Block because, for nearly a century, the corner brick building was the location of H.J. Allen & Sons Hardware. In 2010, Artisans' Corner, formerly McHarris Gifts, opened at the location. Stone Presbyterian Church casts a shadow in each image.

SIDE STREETS AND OTHER ROADS

In the preceding set of images, the shadow cast on the building is that of the Stone Presbyterian Church bell tower, the same spot from where these photographs were taken. In each image, a different event is taking place. The past image shows a large gathering, while the present image depicts the bustling Thursday Clinton Farmers Market. These images exemplify the sense of community that residents have come to associate with Clinton.

In 1884, the Onyan Block was built on the corner of Williams and College Streets. The Williams Street side once housed the Clinton Fire Department's headquarters until the department relocated to North Park Row. The past photograph depicts a hand-pump fire engine in front of the building's now vibrantly painted doors. The current historical signage that provides details of the block's history is evidence of the department's past presence.

Clinton's communication network traces back to the establishment of the first post office in 1802. The area's telecommunication history progressed in 1854 with the first telegraph service, which was followed by the first telephone service in 1897. In 1905, Clinton Home Telephone established its headquarters on Williams Street, occupying the building behind the Onyan Block location. By 1957, the area had implemented a dial service, prompting the telephone company to relocate to Kirkland Avenue.

For over a century, toothaches found their remedy at this small structure on Williams Street. Constructed in the 1870s, the building was used as a dental office. The last dentists to practice at this location were Drs. James Francis and John F. Menard. Currently, the building is a residential space, and Dr. Menard's practice has since relocated to East Park Row. The past image shows a bicycle rider heading south near the former dental office.

At the intersection of Williams and Chestnut Streets stands a prominent house. The residence is on the same grounds where Clara Barton, the founder of the American Red Cross, received an education in 1851. It was known as the White Seminary—the Female Division of the Clinton Liberal Institute. The school closed in 1878, and in 1908, this house was constructed on the site, incorporating four of the original pillars from the seminary.

90—E. F. Torry Residence, Clinton, N. Y.

SIDE STREETS AND OTHER ROADS

Historic Chestnut Street was once home to the most prestigious educational institutions and prominent residences in the area. The photographs depict a view that would have been familiar to the students of the White and Houghton Seminaries. The Houghton Seminary campus on Chestnut Street was first established as the Home Cottage Seminary in 1854. Both images depict the sidewalk that runs along Chestnut Street.

VIEW AT
CLINTON. N.Y.

Established in 1854 as the Home Cottage Seminary, the institution was later renamed the Houghton Seminary in 1861, under the leadership of Marilla Houghton Gallop and Dr. John Chester Gallop. By 1903, the location was no longer used as a school campus. The property was purchased in 1912 and torn down to make way for use as a residence. The present image catches a picturesque sunset, shining through the entrance of the former campus.

St. Marys New Church
Clinton, N.Y.

At the corner of Marvin and Prospect Streets stands St. Mary's Catholic Church, an example of the architectural beauty in the village of Clinton. The current sandstone structure replaced a wooden church from 1854. By the end of 1912, the new St. Mary's Catholic Church was ready for parishioners. The church is complemented by a rectory across the street, emanating its own distinctive Italianate architecture.

The Clinton Union School and Academy, located on Marvin Street, opened in 1893. The school was constructed to accommodate 600 students and house grades first through 12th. When students were later moved to the new school on Chenango Avenue, the Union School continued to operate with elementary classes until 1976. Currently, the former school operates as Marvin Street School Apartments.

High School. Clinton, N. Y.

This view shows the O.J. Burns grocery store on College Street that was featured in chapter two. The *Clinton Courier* wrote that because of his grocery store's location, Burns adopted the marketing slogan, "The Right Man in the Wrong End of Town." Burns was such an instrumental Clintonian that schools and businesses closed for his funeral in 1942.

Over the years, Franklin Avenue, which runs parallel to Marvin Street, has experienced major flooding. This past image from the early days of Clinton displays an instance of flooding with the caption "Overflow of Marvin Brook into Franklin Avenue." Similarly, in 2017, Franklin Avenue was hit by another significant flood, as illustrated in the present image, showing a Clinton Fire Department truck dispatched to pump water.

Clinton Tractor and Implement Company has been steadily growing for over 70 years, offering equipment for agriculture, construction, and residential purposes. Today, the Calidonna family business spans from the intersection of Franklin Avenue to McDonald's on Meadow Street. Notably, the land closest to the fork in the road at the intersection was the original site of Clinton's outdoor skating rink, which was operational from 1926 until 1949.

Side Streets and Other Roads

This strip of stores on Meadow Street has undergone substantial changes to accommodate national pharmacy CVS and northeastern grocery store chain Hannaford. Formerly, the Clinton Shopping Center housed numerous businesses, including a hardware store, a video rental business, a pizzeria, and a diner. The strip has gradually shrunk over time and is now home to locally owned Clinton Wine and Spirits.

The original convenience store and gas station located at 67 Meadow Street started as a small, locally owned business in the 1950s. On April 1, 1980, the store reopened as a Nice N Easy Grocery Shoppe chain. This Meadow Street location was the first Nice N Easy franchise in the area. The store and gas pumps have since been torn down, and at the time of this writing, the area remains an empty lot.

The Clinton Fire Department's Station No. 2 is at 55 Franklin Avenue, between Clinton and Franklin Springs. The location houses a Clinton Fire Department museum dedicated to the over 150 years of history serving Clinton, Kirkland, and the immediate area. The 1860s hand-pump fire engine mentioned at the beginning of this chapter is on display here. The secondary station also features a pavilion used for various events.

Near Clinton Fire Department Station No. 2 is the entrance to Sunset Hill Cemetery. The Old Burying Ground on Kirkland Avenue was the site of many burials until 1855 when it reached capacity. In the mid-1850s, Clinton saw two new cemeteries open—St. Mary's Cemetery and Sunset Hill Cemetery. Most recently, in 2015, a walking path that winds through and around the cemetery called the Path opened. The Path features benches, a shelter with memorial pavers, and a labyrinth.

SIDE STREETS AND OTHER ROADS

Facing the former Nice N Easy Grocery Shoppe stands another family-owned business—Clinton Auto Service. The auto repair shop has been helping local vehicles since 1965, when Fred and Judy Wollin first opened the garage doors for business. In 1994, the repair center expanded to include a car wash, conveniently located adjacent to the repair center on Dwight Avenue. The Clinton Car Wash addition added to the wide range of services offered at the location.

The Town of Kirkland municipal building, where local government officials assemble for meetings, is located near Clinton Auto Service on State Route 12B. The Town of Kirkland's municipal building is situated in front of the highway department barn, and it features offices and a large meeting room where council members and the supervisor convene twice a month to discuss town matters. It is worth noting that Kirkland has a population of just over 10,000 residents, while the village of Clinton is home to approximately 1,900 residents.

SIDE STREETS AND OTHER ROADS

Franklin Springs, located along State Route 12B, just south of Clinton, was once renowned for its mineral and lithia water as well as its iron production. Given its history with iron, the hamlet was once referred to as Franklin Iron Works. This area established a post office in 1867. The building in these photographs once had within it a general store and the post office. In 2011, the post office, which was over 140 years old, closed.

The video rental industry, once a prosperous business, has undergone a significant transformation. In the 1980s, Viddyo was a key player in the local rental business. Viddyo operated from various locations in Clinton, and by the era of DVD rentals, it had established its presence in the Chenango Avenue building. Today, the space where the video rental store once operated now houses Utica Bread and Vit-za Pizza.

Clinton and Kirkland have seen an array of food markets throughout the years, including Victory Market. It opened at this location in 1963, bringing with it a modern supermarket experience. The store operated on West Park Row before moving to this pictured Chenango Avenue spot, across from the Clinton Central School District. Since Victory's closure, the building has had multiple tenants. Great American, another grocery store chain, assumed occupancy in the 1990s before the building transformed into Dollar General.

A noteworthy feature of the Victory Market parking lot and subsequent stores was a centuries-old ginkgo tree. The tree was planted around 1850 and earned a historical marker for its significance. Part of the sign read, "This Ginkgo—'Maiden Hair' tree was planted on the Othniel S. Williams property by the Rural Art Society." The tree was cut down in 2016 due to not having enough space to grow with the pavement around it.

The Clinton Central School District campus features a community brick garden and a monument dedicated to a local hero. Edward Porter Felt, a 1977 graduate of the school, was among the passengers aboard United Airlines Flight 93 when it was hijacked on September 11, 2001, and eventually crashed in Shanksville, Pennsylvania. The monument honors his bravery on that fateful day, and the granite bench depicted in the present image is a part of the memorial.

The Clinton Agway building has a footprint that dates to 1837. Originally, the location served as a canal warehouse during the Chenango Canal's heyday, later transitioning to a feed mill in the early 1900s. By 1927, the site evolved to include a farm supply shop. In 1964, the location became affiliated with the farm supply chain Agway. Today, Clinton Agway now offers a larger selection of goods, including farm supplies, gardening items, home essentials, and hardware.

Clinton House Apartments on Kirkland Avenue is the former site of canal and railroad operations. Here, a canal warehouse was built in 1847. After canal use ended, a railroad freight station replaced it. Pres. Grover Cleveland visited the freight station in July 1887 for dinner and to give a speech during Clinton's centennial celebration. In 1907, the Clinton Knitting Company occupied the site until it was razed in 1969 for Clinton Gardens, a precursor to the current Clinton House Apartments. The former freight station building was moved to an area behind the current apartment complex and is used today by tenants for storage.

Local newspapers have traditionally been and remain the heartbeat of small towns. The significance of local journalism is not lost on this writer, who has firsthand experience covering Clinton news as a reporter. The *Clinton Courier,* founded in 1846, was the primary source for hyperlocal news in Clinton and Kirkland until its closure in 2015. At the time this past photograph was taken, the *Courier* was operating out of this Kirkland Avenue building. The site now accommodates offices and apartments.

Where North Park Row and Kirkland Avenue meet stands the Hayes National Bank building. Next to the bank, in the past image, is Dawes Market, mentioned in chapter one. Hayes moved to this location in 1896, originally operating out of Seth Hastings's 1808 homestead. Prior to bank use, the Hastings house was utilized by the Clinton Female Seminary in 1814, according to *A Century of Schools in Clinton* by Helen Neilson Rudd. In the 1930s, the bank underwent a significant renovation, leading to the current version known today. NBT Bank currently occupies this building.

On Kirkland Avenue near the Old Burying Ground stands what was once known as the Royce Mansion. Originally a large homestead, it became a school for young women called both the Royce Seminary and Clinton Female Seminary. The leadership of sisters Nancy and Eliza Royce attracted students to the seminary from various regions of the state and Canada. The school closed in 1856. Presently, the historic building serves as an apartment complex.

SIDE STREETS AND OTHER ROADS

Merab Tuttle, the first person to die in the new Clinton settlement, drowned in the Oriskany Creek in 1788. Tuttle's original burial site near the present Village Green had soil that was too wet. This prompted the use of land on Kirkland Avenue for the burial, now known as the Old Burying Ground. Multiple American Revolutionary War veterans are buried here, along with Clinton founder Capt. Moses Foote. The last burial here was in 1920.

A former Gene Oliver garage, located adjacent to the Old Bury Ground on Norton Avenue, now houses Hale Transportation, a popular charter bus and transportation company. In the 1960s, Utica-Rome Bus Company, also a charter bus company, started operating from this location. By 2006, Hale's Bus Garage was established, serving as a precursor to Hale Transportation. Over time, owner Stephen Hale has transformed this location into a state-of-the-art facility.

SIDE STREETS AND OTHER ROADS

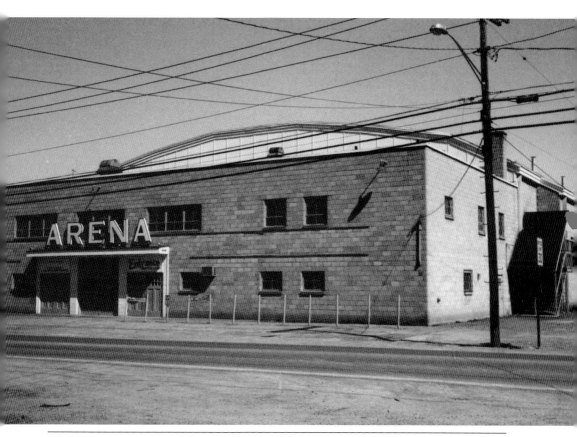

Clinton is a hockey town so immersed in the game that the community took home Kraft Hockeyville USA in 2018, bringing with the title win an NHL hockey game played at the Clinton Arena, funding for rink improvements, and a visit from the Stanley Cup to the historic venue. The building pictured represents the second iteration of the Clinton Arena, as the original rink was destroyed by fire in 1953. The Clinton Comets hockey team called this arena home from 1949 to 1973.

Norton Avenue, situated opposite the Clinton Arena, is home to the Jack Boynton Community Pool, which opened in 1957. Boynton was a prominent member of the community and an editor and owner of the *Clinton Courier*. Prior to the community pool, residents sometimes resorted to cooling off in the Franklin Iron Works blast furnace pond in Franklin Springs or the Oriskany Creek on hot days. This Norton Avenue pool has been a summer destination for generations, offering a place to cool down and quality swimming lessons.

Another street off Kirkland Avenue is McBride Avenue, which has been home to Clinton Collision since the late 1970s. McBride Avenue was a bustling area with the establishment of the Clinton Canning Company in 1892. In 1911, the *Clinton Courier* wrote that the factory "is the busiest place in the community . . . running practically night and day to care for the rapidly maturing pea crop." Most of the buildings affiliated with the factory have been razed.

Located just beyond the village limits on Kirkland Avenue is this historic residence that dates to 1797. Founder Moses Foote's son-in-law Barnabas Pond built this house. Notably, some of Pond's land was used for the Old Burying Ground, and he was responsible for digging the grave of Merab Tuttle, the village's first death. In recognition of Pond's home being one of the oldest in Clinton, a historic marker was placed at the site in 1974.

Located farther up Kirkland Avenue from the Barnabas Pond homestead stands an unassuming house, which, according to the *Clinton Courier*, dates to 1789, making it one of the oldest structures still standing in the town of Kirkland. Also interesting is the original owner of the home, Jesse Curtiss, who built it when he was 22 years old during the year of great food scarcity in the area. Curtiss, who was a county legislator, served as the town supervisor for nearly 30 years.

Back in the village of Clinton, the corner of Beatty Avenue and Utica Street was once the site of the street's first gas station. Arthur Thomas built the business in 1925 at the corner, adjacent to Sherman Brook. The location transitioned into an auto repair shop in the mid-1960s, with ownership changes over the years, until ceasing operations in approximately 1989. The original structure has since been demolished. Next door at 66 Utica Street is the well-known Clinton Pottery.

SIDE STREETS AND OTHER ROADS

A national coffee chain has operated from the site of a former gas station at 35 Utica Street since 1999. According to an advertisement in the *Clinton Courier* from October 1989, the X-Tra Mart at this spot was preparing for a grand reopening. However, almost a decade later, in December 1998, the building was undergoing a conversion to Dunkin' Donuts. The *Courier* also reported that a house at 1 Taylor Avenue was demolished for the coffee chain's parking lot.

Parallel to the former X-Tra Mart was a historic gas station and car service center. The second gas station on Utica Street opened in 1928 at 33 Utica Street under the proprietorship of Fred Suppe, who later transformed it into a car dealership. After Suppe retired in 1971, the site became a Mobil station. Eventually, it became a Nice N Easy Grocery Shoppe. Cliff's Local Market occupies the site today.

SIDE STREETS AND OTHER ROADS

The property at 26 Utica Street in the village of Clinton is of historical interest because it was the boyhood home of Pres. Grover Cleveland. While here, Cleveland attended Clinton Grammar School, aspiring to attend Hamilton College. His sister Rose attended Houghton Seminary, later becoming a teacher there. It has been said that Rose once fell into the Village Green fountain. Later in life, Rose served as her brother's first lady until his marriage to Frances Folsom, marking the first presidential marriage in the White House.

These images show a rare example of a demolition within village limits. In the early years of Clinton, several structures, such as the Park House, were dismantled, making way for Lumbard Hall, which is located across the street from these former buildings. In 1994, discussions were held to demolish 2–4 Utica Street and another on East Park Row to expand parking for the car dealership Cawley's. The plan was eventually approved. An auto parts store uses the parking lot today.

Upon reaching the intersection where Utica Street becomes East Park Row, the road directly ahead is Fountain Street. Notably, 4 Fountain Street, constructed in 1924, was formerly the Clinton Grange, a farmers' association organization. During the 1930s, the building housed the Clinton Theater. In 1971, it was known as Cannonball Cinema. By the 2000s, the theater had ceased operation and was eventually converted into office space.

DISCOVER THOUSANDS OF LOCAL HISTORY BOOKS FEATURING MILLIONS OF VINTAGE IMAGES

Arcadia Publishing, the leading local history publisher in the United States, is committed to making history accessible and meaningful through publishing books that celebrate and preserve the heritage of America's people and places.

Find more books like this at
www.arcadiapublishing.com

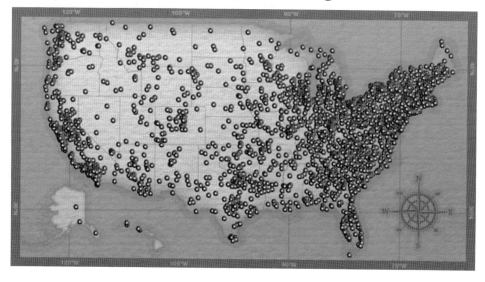

Search for your hometown history, your old stomping grounds, and even your favorite sports team.